Growing Dwarf Bulbs

A Wisley Handbook

Growing
Dwarf Bulbs

JACK ELLIOTT

Cassell

The Royal Horticultural Society

THE ROYAL HORTICULTURAL SOCIETY

Cassell Educational Limited
Villiers House, 41/47 Strand
London WC2N 5JE
for the Royal Horticultural Society

First published 1988
Second edition 1993

British Library Cataloguing in Publication Data
A catalogue record for this book is available from the British Library

ISBN 0–304–32058–7

Photographs by Jack Elliott, Photos Horticultural and the
Harry Smith Collection

Phototypesetting by RGM Associates, Southport
Printed in Hong Kong by Wing King Tong Co. Ltd

Cover: *Iris reticulata* 'Harmony' is one of the most reliable and freely
increasing of the Reticulata irises.
p. 2: The beautiful *Erythronium oregonum* thrives in semi-shade.
    Photographs by Photos Horticultural
p. 1: Robust *Colchicum agrippinum*, with well-tesselated flowers, is thought
to be a garden hybrid of *C. variegatum*.
Back cover: *Crocus tommasinianus* is the most rapidly increasing spring-
flowering species and suitable for naturalising.
    Photographs by the Harry Smith Collection

Contents

Introduction 7

General Cultivation 8
Where to grow dwarf bulbs 8
In grass 8
In raised beds or a rock garden 10
In borders and flower beds 11
In shady situations 12
In containers 13
Under glass 13
Propagation 15
Pests and diseases 16

Crocus 18
Autumn-flowering 19
Winter- and spring-flowering 20

Colchicum 23

Galanthus 25

Leucojum 27

Iris 29
Reticulata irises 29
Juno irises 31

Narcissus 34

Tulipa 39

Dwarf Bulbs for Autumn and Winter 43
September to November 43
December to February 45

Dwarf Bulbs for Spring 48
Shade-lovers 48
Sun-lovers 53

Dwarf Bulbs for Summer 59

Index 64

Introduction

Few plants give better value in the garden than dwarf bulbs. They make up for their small size by their freedom of flowering and ease of cultivation, needing the minimum of attention after planting and increasing happily if left undisturbed. There is a vast range of dwarf bulbs, most of them readily obtainable and inexpensive, and they are suitable for every position from moist shade to hot dry situations. By choosing some of the less well-known ones, the bulb season, which is generally concentrated in March and April, can be extended throughout the year, including the difficult months of late autumn and winter.

This book describes a selection of the most rewarding dwarf bulbs, both the familiar and the more unusual, and gives guidance on their cultivation. Individual chapters are devoted to the major genera – crocus, colchicum, galanthus, leucojum, iris, narcissus, tulip – followed by chapters on other bulbs grouped according to their season of flowering, from autumn to summer.

The term bulb has been used here to embrace not only true bulbs, but corms (e.g. crocus) and tubers (e.g. anemone) which are commonly thought of as "bulbs" and behave in a similar way. However, definitely rhizomatous plants (e.g. certain irises) have been excluded. Height limits have not been applied too strictly, but the majority of plants will be under 12 in. (30 cm) tall and all are hardy in the south of England. A few suggestions are also made for growing them under glass, in an unheated greenhouse or frame, where some of the choicer bulbs can benefit from perfect conditions. All the plants mentioned should be available from trade sources and especially from the numerous bulb specialists who advertise in the gardening press.

Opposite: *Allium murrayanum* is an easily grown onion which flowers in summer

General Cultivation

The majority of bulbs are offered for sale in a dry semi-dormant state in the autumn. These should be planted as early as possible, at a depth depending on the size of the bulb and the type of soil, from about 3 in. (8 cm) for the smaller ones to 8 in. (20 cm) for the larger. The importance of good drainage is stressed later (see p.10) and in heavy soil it is helpful to put coarse sand round the bulbs when planting them. In a few cases, notably cyclamen and snowdrops, the bulbs are usually sold in growth, packed in peat or other moist material, and should be planted immediately. If the ground is frozen, it is advisable to keep them temporarily in pots until conditions have improved. Other summer- and autumn-flowering bulbs may be obtainable in spring or summer and should always be planted as soon as possible.

Most bulbs need only the minimum of care to ensure their survival from year to year and can be left undisturbed after planting. However, some, such as daffodils, will increase so freely that they become overcrowded within about three years, resulting in loss of vigour and fewer flowers. The bulbs should then be lifted during the dormant period, preferably in August or early September, divided and replanted individually in new positions. If they are replaced in the same soil, a general fertilizer such as bonemeal should be incorporated.

As with other garden plants, the first essential for success is a well-prepared soil with adequate nutrients. Bonemeal is an excellent fertilizer, dug in at the time of initial planting, or forked into the surface of the soil as a subsequent top dressing before the bulbs are due to appear. Freshly manured ground should be avoided and must be left at least six months before bulbs are planted.

WHERE TO GROW DWARF BULBS

In grass

Large bold daffodils look their best when growing naturally in rough grass; but anyone who has seen the sheets of *Narcissus bulbocodium* in the alpine meadow at the RHS Garden, Wisley, or at the Savill Garden, Windsor Great Park, will appreciate that their smaller relatives can also be used in this way. Unfortunately,

The native snake's head, *Fritillaria meleagris*, establishes itself happily in grass and increases from seed

the number of dwarf bulbs which can cope with the competition of grass is limited mainly to the more vigorous ones. Among them are *Narcissus bulbocodium*, *N. cyclamineus* and their cultivars, *Scilla bifolia*, Dutch crocuses, *Crocus chrysanthus* hybrids, *C. tommasinianus*, *Fritillaria meleagris*, *F. pyrenaica* and grape hyacinths (*Muscari*) in the spring; *Leucojum aestivum* in the summer; and *Crocus speciosus*, *C. kotschyanus*, *Colchicum autumnale* and *C. speciosum* in the autumn.

It is essential to plant the bulbs at least twice their own depth and to leave the grass uncut until their leaves have started to die down. There are various planting methods. A long-handled bulb planter, designed to be pressed down with the foot, is ideal for the larger bulbs (and much better than the hand-held instrument, which requires considerable pressure and is almost unusable unless the ground is very soft). For small bulbs, sections of turf can be lifted with a spade and the underlying soil loosened, the bulbs planted and the turf replaced; alternatively, a garden fork with broad tines can be used, pushing it into the ground and moving it backwards and forwards to widen the holes, planting the bulbs one to each hole and finally covering with a little loose soil. Care must be taken with this method to vary the position and direction of the fork, so that the bulbs do not appear to be in straight lines: an effect of informal drifts should always be the aim. Planting should be done as soon as the bulbs are available, although it is easier after a period of wet weather. It is also a good idea to cut the grass just before planting.

Bulbs in grass will benefit from occasional top dressings of a general fertilizer, such as Growmore, in February. However, the most important factor in ensuring their continued vigour is to let their leaves die down before cutting the grass. This will be several weeks after they have finished flowering and they will look very untidy. The grass can usually be cut in June, when most of the spring-flowering bulbs will be over, and repeated once or twice before the autumn-flowering crocuses and colchicums come into growth. If you are also hoping for increase from self-sowing, for example, from *Fritillaria meleagris* or *Narcissus bulbocodium*, then the grass cutting must be delayed even longer, until the seed capsules have emptied, frequently two or three weeks after the leaves have died down.

In raised beds or a rock garden

Most bulbs will benefit from the same soil preparation as alpine plants, good drainage being the vital ingredient for both. This can be achieved by raising the bed a little above the surrounding ground and incorporating plenty of horticultural grit in the soil. Although not essential, a top dressing of the same grit helps to conserve moisture and prevent small plants from being battered by heavy rain. (For further information about raised beds, see the Wisley Handbook, *Alpines the Easy Way*.)

A raised bed can accommodate a wide range of dwarf bulbs and alpines, which are small enough to be in scale with each other, whereas bulbs are often lost among larger perennials and shrubs, unless kept well to the front of a border. The alpine plants can also help to prolong the display. Wherever bulbs are grown, however, the question arises of how to fill the bare patches when they are dormant in summer. It is often recommended that they should be planted under low carpeting plants and the rock garden is the best place to try this, using such ground-covering plants as thymes, raoulias and some of the smaller campanulas and phlox. Although in theory this makes maximum use of the space available, it presents problems because many of these plants root as they run, so that the bulbs face severe competition. In addition, the dying foliage of more vigorous bulbs can detract from the overall appearance. Perhaps the best compromise is to place the bulbs in groups between plants which spread widely from a

Osteospermums can be recomended for planting with bulbs, to follow on after these have finished

central rootstock during the growing season and then die back, or can be cut back, for the winter – for instance, the hardier osteospermums, *O. jucundum* *(Dimorphotheca barberiae)* 'Compacta' and *O. ecklonis* 'Prostrata', *Convolvulus sabatius* and *Sphaeralcea munroana*. Alternatively, the bulbs can be planted between rock garden shrubs which make most of their growth after the bulbs have flowered, such as *Zauschneria californica*, *Ceratostigma willmottianum* and the smaller potentillas.

In borders and flower beds

Much of what has been said about the rock garden applies on a larger scale to planting in beds and borders, especially if the soil is light and well-drained. Most bulbs favour a sunny position and are therefore best planted near the front of a border, where they will not be shaded too heavily by other plants, at least during the growing and flowering season, and where they can also be seen. After the bulbs have died down, partial shade will have little effect on their growth. In fact, all but the most ardent sun-lovers may be planted in the dappled shade of deciduous shrubs and small trees and will appreciate the drier conditions maintained by the tree and shrub roots in summer, as well as the lack of disturbance to the soil.

In a herbaceous border which is regularly cultivated, bulbs may be less successful and can even be a nuisance. However, groups of the more vigorous ones can be planted between herbaceous perennials to advance the flowering season in the earlier part of the year. Many tender perennials have gained popularity recently, because they will grow rapidly from cuttings overwintered under glass – for example, the osteospermums already mentioned and other *Osteospermum* species and hybrids, gazanias and verbenas. These are ideal for associating with bulbs, since they can be cut back in the autumn, after which they may survive the winter. Annuals and bedding plants can be used in a similar way, if one is prepared for the work involved.

Although most rose-growers seem to frown upon any interplanting of roses in formal beds, it is certainly possible to grow dwarf bulbs there, preferably choosing those which are unlikely to need lifting, dividing or other attentions that might disturb the rose roots. Shrub rose enthusiasts will probably have fewer qualms about interplanting, if this can be done before the roses have become too well-established and filled the bed with roots.

In shady situations

A number of bulbs are natives of woodland and will flourish in shady parts of the garden, so long as the soil is enriched with plenty of humus, peat or leaf mould. Most woodland plants also like abundant moisture and these shade-loving bulbs are no exception, although a few of the more vigorous kinds, especially *Cyclamen coum* and *C. hederifolium*, may grow and even increase in dry shade.

Trilliums and erythroniums need moist woodland conditions, which are also enjoyed by many anemones, snowdrops, cyclamen, certain fritillaries and some narcissus. Unfortunately, shade, whether from walls and buildings or from trees and shrubs, often results in poor dry soil and the incorporation of organic matter is essential. The ground close to a wall can be very dry and may require extra watering as well as extra humus. The success of planting under trees, hedges and shrubs depends mainly on the extent of their roots, which deprive smaller plants of both food and moisture. Tall deep-rooting trees like oak provide perfect natural conditions, casting a light shade without impoverishing the surrounding soil. However, many other trees and shrubs have greedy roots (birch and privet are particularly bad) and bulbs planted beneath them should be given additional fertilizer, such as bonemeal or Growmore, forked into the surface in early spring.

In containers

Many dwarf bulbs thrive in troughs and sinks, together with alpines, and share their liking for sharply drained soil and an open sunny site. Their dainty attractions can also be appreciated in such a setting. The smallest and least invasive bulbs should be chosen, so that they do not dominate or overwhelm their neighbours, and those with unobtrusive foliage which does not look too untidy after flowering are preferable. The dwarfest crocuses, cyclamen and rhodohypoxis would be good candidates.

Many of the easily grown dwarf bulbs can be used to provide early colour in ornamental containers, such as pots and urns on a patio and window boxes. The commoner crocuses, daffodils, grape hyacinths, scillas, Reticulata irises and tulips are all suitable. If they are to be followed by other plants, they should be lifted when the leaves begin to die down and then either planted out in the garden, or kept in a cool dry place for replanting in the autumn in the containers.

Under glass

Although most of the bulbs described in this book will succeed in the open garden and few require protection from cold, some can be grown to advantage under glass, either in an unheated greenhouse or in a frame. This shelters them from excessive rain in winter, keeps the blooms in pristine condition, which is especially valuable with very early-flowering or tiny plants, and provides the relatively dry dormant period after flowering to which so many bulbs are accustomed in their natural habitats. Among those recommended for cultivation under glass are small-flowered colchicums, Juno irises, the slightly tender cyclamen, Jonquil narcissus, less common species of crocus, leucojum, tulip and fritillary and such little-known genera as *Calochortus* and *Habranthus*.

There are two methods of growing bulbs under glass – either in pots or planted in a bed – and in both cases they can be covered with a frame or Dutch lights or kept in a cold greenhouse. A suitable compost for the pots is John Innes No. 2, with a third of its bulk of grit added; alternatively, a home-made compost can be prepared, consisting of two parts loam, preferably sterilized, one part peat and one and a half parts grit, plus 8 oz (225 g) John Innes base fertilizer and 4 oz (110 g) lime to the bushel (8 gallons; 36 litres). A well-drained peat-based compost, with extra grit incorporated, is another possibility. Clay or plastic pots may be used: the former minimize the risk of overwatering, but are best plunged in sand to prevent them drying out too quickly.

13

Above: 'Cream Beauty' (left), one of the several robust hybrids of *Crocus chrysanthus*; *Calochortus venustus* (right) a choice summer-flowering bulb for a warm spot

Below: *Cyclamen coum* and winter aconites, *Eranthis hyemalis*, enjoy the dappled shade of shrubs and trees and both self-sow freely

The bulbs should be potted as soon as they can be obtained in late summer, ideally in September or early October, and planted at about three times their own depth or, for large bulbs, about a third of the way up the pot. After planting, they should be top dressed with grit and kept watered until growth dies down in May. Many of the trickier bulbs, such as some fritillaries and tulips, benefit from a summer drying off period, without any water at all. They can then be repotted if they are becoming over-crowded, or top dressed with fresh potting compost, before being started into growth again in September.

For planting bulbs in a bed with overhead protection, be it in a frame or cold greenhouse, a similar compost is suitable, again ensuring that it is well-drained. In a frame, the bed should be raised above ground level to improve drainage. This will create a "bulb frame", which is simply a raised bed covered with frame lights. Many bulbs increase and grow more vigorously if planted in a bed, the main disadvantage being the difficulty of retrieving them if they need to be lifted when dormant. To overcome this, growers often put the choicer bulbs in plastic lattice pots (of the type used for aquatic plants) plunged in the bed; another solution is to separate the different groups with vertical tiles or slates. After the first year, bonemeal should be forked into the surface every spring.

PROPAGATION

Most of the common bulbs increase freely of their own accord, by splitting into two or more bulbs, like many daffodils, or by forming small bulbils around the base of the parent bulb, a feature of many Reticulata irises and fritillaries. These may be carefully separated or detached and planted individually. On the other hand, many of the less common bulbs do not increase readily in this way, but do set seed.

Although gardeners seem reluctant to grow bulbs from seed, the technique is not difficult and requires only a modicum of patience. The majority of bulbs will flower within three years of sowing and few take longer than five years – time which passes quickly if more species are sown each year, so that there are always new arrivals to be enjoyed.

Seed usually ripens by midsummer and should be sown as early as possible in the autumn, in John Innes seed compost or a peat-based compost with good drainage. Sow the seeds fairly thinly, just cover them with compost and finish with a layer of chippings at least ¼ in. (0.5 cm) thick. Put the pots outside in a shady place and keep moist until the seeds germinate, after which they can be

15

Like many Reticulata irises, *I. histriodes* 'Major' increases freely from offsets

brought into a frame or cold greenhouse or at least be exposed to more light. The seedlings can normally be kept in the original pots for two growing seasons, allowing them to dry off when the foliage dies down and starting to water again in September. Some seed, especially if it is not sown until after Christmas, may not germinate for a further year and in this case the compost should be kept moist throughout. After two years, the young bulbs can be either repotted in the same way as adult bulbs or, if they are reasonably large, planted in the garden.

PESTS AND DISEASES

Pest and diseases generally cause few problems with bulbous plants, especially when they are grown in the open garden, but some of the more common are listed here.

Slugs can damage young growth, especially in damp conditions, and underground they may damage the bulbs themselves. Any of the slug killers available, as pellets or liquid preparations, can be used effectively.

Aphids are rarely troublesome except under glass. They should be treated as soon as they are seen with dimethoate, heptenophos or pirimicarb, since they can weaken the plants and are respon-

16

sible for the spread of viruses (see below). Red spider mite only affects bulbs grown under glass, particularly if the atmosphere has been allowed to become very dry. If a severe infestation occurs, frequent spraying with pirimiphos-methyl, malathion or dimethoate will be necessary. Alternatively, the predatory mite *Phytoseiulus persimilis* can be introduced.

Vine weevil can be a serious pest with pot-grown bulbs, especially cyclamen and begonia. Sterilized compost should be used and, if the grubs, which have curved white bodies and brown heads, are seen, the compost should be removed from around the bulbs and the grubs killed. Fresh compost should then be used incorporating gamma-HCH dust. A nematode drench (*Heterorhabditis* sp.) applied in late summer can give good control. Also a vine weevil predator is available for severe infestations.

Lily beetle is becoming increasingly common in certain parts of the country, notably Surrey and the surrounding counties, and can cause severe damage to the leaves of fritillaries, as well as lilies. The beetles, which are bright red and about $\frac{1}{3}$ in. (8 mm) long, and their reddish grubs covered in black excrement should be picked off whenever they are seen. Regular spraying with permethrin, pirimiphos-methyl or fenitrothion is also effective.

Two other pests, the large narcissus bulb fly and stem and bulb eelworm, are difficult to control as amateur insecticides are ineffective. Birds and mice can be destructive in some gardens and, as crocuses are particularly prone, control is discussed on p. 18.

Botrytis occasionally affects bulbs, especially under glass, fritillaries, tulips and irises being the most frequently attacked. The earliest sign is usually the development of grey spots on the leaves, which spread rapidly to the whole plant. Spraying with benomyl or carbendazim is normally effective.

Virus disease is a difficult problem which is more likely to worry the specialist grower than the average gardener. The difficulty arises partly from the fact that commercial stocks of certain plants, of which lilies and irises are notorious, may already be infected without showing typical symptoms. Unfortunately, the virus can be spread by aphids from these to more susceptible plants, causing streaking of the leaves or flowers and gradual loss of vigour. Micropropagation methods have made it possible to achieve virus-free stocks and plants grown from seed are also virus-free, which may eventually ensure that all stocks are healthy. In the meantime, obviously affected plants should be destroyed and regular spraying against aphids should be undertaken to prevent spread of the disease. (See also p. 29 for ink disease.)

Crocus

Crocuses are among the most widely grown dwarf bulbs for the spring garden, but their popularity rests mainly on the large-flowered Dutch hybrids, listed in a wide range of varieties in every bulb catalogue. These are easily grown in sun or partial shade in most soils and will even thrive in grass, as long as the leaves are allowed to die down before cutting it. Most catalogues give adequate descriptions of the colours and variations in flowering period and individual descriptions would be superfluous here.

The genus is a large one and the numerous species now in cultivation have a delicate charm lacking in the familiar Dutch hybrids. Many are easily grown and sufficiently prodigal in their increase to provide good patches of colour in the garden, while those requiring a little extra care can easily be grown in a frame or unheated greenhouse. Few genera can provide colour for such a long period, from August until May.

The majority of crocuses grow well in an open sunny situation in well-drained soil. A rock garden is ideal, but any position where they can be appreciated in spite of their small size is suitable, especially if the drainage has been improved by incorporating extra grit.

Many crocuses increase well by division and some will self-sow themselves around after a year or two. However, it is always worthwhile looking for seed of the less common species, which can be expected to flower in three or four years from sowing. The ripe seed capsules are frequently hidden at ground level and need searching for among the dying leaves.

Diseases are rarely a problem, but pests can be troublesome. Whether in the garden or under glass, the corms seem to be particularly appetizing to mice and in some woodland gardens are equally popular with squirrels. An enthusiastic mouse-catching cat can work wonders, otherwise traps may be effective. In a frame, mice can be kept at bay by lining it with fine mesh netting. Birds are another nuisance and often treat crocuses, especially yellow varieties, in the same way as primroses and polyanthus, nipping through the flower stems at or above ground level. Apart from avoiding crocuses which are likely targets, the only answer is bird netting or, less conspicuously, black cotton.

The following list contains a selection of species and cultivars which are obtainable from the trade and which should succeed in the open garden. For the ever-increasing number of crocus enthusiasts, further information about the rarer species can be obtained from the more specialist books available.

AUTUMN-FLOWERING

Many of the autumn-flowering crocuses resemble the colchicums, in that they produce their flowers before the leaves appear, in October and November, generally in shades of pale to deep lavender or white and often with conspicuous orange anthers. This description fits the two vigorous large-flowered species most commonly seen in the catalogues – *Crocus speciosus*, and *C. kotschyanus* (frequently listed as *C. zonatus*). The latter has pale lilac flowers with two yellow spots at the base of each segment, while its variety *leucopharynx* (*C. karduchorum*) has a pure white throat and tube and is one of the most beautiful of all crocuses, increasing well in the garden. *C. speciosus* is more variable and several cultivars have been named, including the white 'Albus', deep violet 'Oxonian' and the very large, pale 'Aitchisonii'.

Also similar in their colour range and absence of leaves at flowering time are *Crocus medius*, *C. nudiflorus* and *C. pulchellus*. *C. nudiflorus* has darker flowers than the others and is unusual in being stoloniferous, so that it usually builds up a colony quite quickly. 'Zephyr', a cultivar of *C. pulchellus*, is very vigorous and has exceptionally pale flowers.

One species deserving special mention is *Crocus banaticus*, known as *C. iridiflorus* in the past because of the intriguing iris-like flowers, in which the inner segments are small and tend to curve in, whereas the outer segments spread outwards or recurve. The beauty of the pale lavender flowers is enhanced by the conspicuous, branching, white anthers. Although still expensive, this is an easy plant in a situation which does not get too dry and it increases freely.

Several autumn-flowering crocuses develop their leaves to a greater or lesser degree by the time the flowers appear, giving an appearance quite different from the naked flowers of those already described. The colour range is again similar. The saffron crocus, *Crocus sativus*, is typical, having abundant leaves and lilac flowers heavily veined with purple, with striking red anthers. Unfortunately, the flowers are not readily produced in Britain and the smaller-flowered *C. cartwrightianus* and robust *C. serotinus* subsp. *salzmannii* are more floriferous plants. Into this group, of which the nomenclature is confusing, probably falls the crocus called in catalogues *C. asturicus* 'Atropurpureus', with an excellent deep purple flower.

Another species occasionally offered is *Crocus laevigatus*, which varies considerably from white to lavender but usually has beautiful dark veining. Its much more vigorous cultivar, 'Fontenayi', is easily grown and flowers into December. The finest of these crocuses is *C. goulimyi*, which was discovered in southern Greece as recently as 1955 and is rapidly becoming a garden favourite. It has a somewhat globular, pale lavender flower with a white throat and an exceptionally long tube. There is also a lovely pure white variety and both will increase happily in the garden.

There are several other white autumn-flowering species. The two easiest and most readily available are *Crocus ochroleucus* and *C. hadriaticus*, the former having a yellow throat.

WINTER- AND SPRING-FLOWERING

The crocuses already described flower mainly in October and November and may produce occasional flowers in December, to coincide with the earliest of the winter- and spring-flowering species. There are three that can be relied upon to start flowering in January in normal weather conditions. *Crocus imperati* is usually the first – a beautiful plant whose large flowers are deep purple when they open in the sunshine, but buff-coloured with dark feathering on the outside of the unopened buds. A striking contrast is provided by *C. fleischeri*, which has small, pure white flowers with prominent, large, red anthers. Although delicate in appearance, it withstands the weather well and is a good garden plant. The earliest of the yellow crocuses generally starts flowering in January. This is *C. ancyrensis*, with small flowers sometimes marked brown on the outside of the petals.

Depending on the weather, the main flowering period of crocuses is February to March, with a few late species carrying on the display in April. Following *Crocus ancyrensis*, there are a number of others with deep yellow flowers, some with conspicuous brown or purple markings. The popular *C. flavus* (*C. aureus*) is very vigorous and freely increasing, especially in the clone generally

Opposite, top: *Crocus speciosus* (left) and *C. kotschyanus* (right) are the best-known autumn-flowering species

Centre: *C. fleischeri* (left) and *C. ancyrensis* (right) are especially valuable for their winter blooms

Bottom: *C.* 'Hubert Edelsten' (left) and *C. alexandri* (right) are both distinctive for their colouring

available in the trade, which has larger flowers than the wild species. Unfortunately, this is the crocus most likely to have its flowers demolished by birds.

A clear yellow species with large flowers, *Crocus chrysanthus* is best known as the parent of many excellent robust hybrids, such as 'Blue Pearl' and 'Blue Bird' among the blues, 'Cream Beauty', a soft, creamy yellow, 'E. A. Bowles' and 'Gypsy Girl' in deeper yellow and the white 'Snow Bunting' and 'Ladykiller', the latter having deep purple on the outside of the petals. *C. olivieri* has deep yellow or orange flowers, normally unmarked, although the more frequently offered subspecies *balansae*, which is almost identical, is heavily streaked with brown.

There are several spring-flowering species in shades of lavender or purple, often with attractive darker feathering. The commonest by far is *Crocus tommasinianus*, which has lavender-blue flowers with white throats and increases so prodigiously by division and by seed that its planting may be regretted, except perhaps in grass. However, these strictures do not apply to the white form, 'Albus', or the dark purple 'Whitwell Purple', which are both well worth growing.

The popular *Crocus dalmaticus* is pale purple with a brownish tinge on the outside. The variable *C. vernus* generally has flowers in shades of lavender, while the equally variable *C. sieberi* tends to have a deep orange throat. In the variety *tricolor*, this is separated form the pale purple tips by a white band – a dramatic colour combination – and the hybrid 'Hubert Edelsten' also has an unusual mixture of white and reddish purple.

Two species with pale purple flowers notable for their dark feathering, particularly in bud, are the very similar *Crocus minimus* and *C. corsicus*. The most obvious difference to the gardener is that *C. minimus* is one of the earliest and *C. corsicus* one of the latest to flower. Of the botanically complicated *C. biflorus*, nurserymen generally offer *C. biflorus* subsp. *biflorus*, which is white with extensive purple streaking on the outside of the segments, and two other subspecies – the striking *alexandri*, with a dark violet band on the reverse, and *weldenii*, in which the outside of the segments is suffused with brownish grey.

Colchicum

Although commonly called autumn crocus, this genus differs from crocus both botanically and horticulturally. Whereas crocuses belong to the iris family and have three stamens and a symmetrical corm, colchicums belong to the lily family and have six stamens and an irregular elongated corm with a flattened projection below the point of exit of the roots, which is at the side of the corm. From the gardener's point of view, the most important distinction is that the leaves of most autumn-flowering colchicums are very large and, appearing in the spring after the flowers, persist late into the summer. The colour too is often a shade of pink, deeper or paler, which is not often seen in crocuses. Colchicums may be propagated by division of the corms or from seed.

Most of the commonly available large-leaved colchicums flower from August to October or November and are easy to grow in sun or semi-shade, but their placing in the garden is less easy than with crocuses whose leaves are insignificant and disappear quickly. A compromise is needed between a position where the comparatively small crocus-like flowers can be appreciated and one where the persistent cabbage-like leaves cannot damage other low plants. The most vigorous colchicums will grow in rough grass, but mowing or scything then has to be left very late, until the foliage has died down. The ideal situation is probably towards the front of a shrub border, where no other ground-covering plants are used. In addition to the well-known colchicums of this kind, there are several small-leaved delicate species, mostly spring-flowering, for which cultivation under glass is advisable.

The two commonest species offered in catalogues are *Colchicum autumnale* and *C. speciosum*. The former is the one often known confusingly as autumn crocus or meadow saffron and has lilac-pink flowers, but there are white and double forms, *album* and 'Pleniflorum', as well as the closely related, deep purple *C. atropurpureum*. *C. speciosum* is a magnificent species with much larger, pink flowers and a number of named forms, of which 'Album' is an exceptionally fine (and expensive) white. *C. cilicium* resembles a larger-flowered *C. autumnale* with very big leaves and *C. macrophyllum* is similar with perhaps the largest leaves of all, up to 20 in. (50 cm) long and 6 in. (15 cm) wide. Some species have a darker chequering on the segments, which adds to their

Colchicum speciosum (left) and its exquisite white-flowered form, 'Album' (right); the flowers are showy enough to compensate for the large leaves which follow

attractiveness. This is well marked in *Colchicum agrippinum, C. bivonae (C. bowlesianum)* and *C. sibthorpii.*

A number of colchicums have smaller flowers and relatively insignificant leaves, but they are less easy to grow and more liable to be damaged by the weather. However, they make excellent pot or frame plants. They include two similar autumn-flowering species – *Colchicum boissieri* and *C. cupanii*, which both have small, unchequered, pink flowers with a white tube and throat, the latter being unusual in producing leaves at the same time. The small spring-flowering species are generally too frail to be grown outside and only available from specialist nurseries. Among them are the rare *Colchicum luteum*, unique in the genus in having deep yellow flowers, and *C. hungaricum*, one of the most reliable dwarf species, bearing palest pink or white flowers with conspicuous chocolate-coloured anthers from January to March.

Galanthus

Most gardeners grow and love snowdrops, whether in occasional groups tucked beneath shrubs and soon forgotten after flowering, or naturalized by the thousand in woodland. The true galanthophile recognizes some 20 species of *Galanthus* and perhaps over 100 varieties, often varying only slightly in size, shape and in the number of green markings on the segments. Generally speaking, they are 3 to 5 in. (8–12 cm) high. A few of the more distinct kinds are described here and the enthusiast should refer to the specialist literature and catalogues.

Snowdrops generally grow best in partial or full shade under trees or shrubs, as long as the soil is not too dry, although a few prefer a sunnier position in well-drained soil. Unlike so many shade-lovers, they thrive on alkaline soils. They differ from the majority of bulbs in establishing most successfully when they are planted in growth or "in the green", preferably after flowering; for this reason, the cheap dry bulbs available for planting in autumn may not prove a good investment. Snowdrops are easily propagated from seed or by dividing clumps of bulbs.

The season starts, surprisingly, in the autumn, with *Galanthus nivalis* subsp. *reginae-olgae* (sometimes offered as *G. corcyrensis* or *G. reginae-olgae*). The flowers appear before the leaves in the earliest forms and it grows well in the open garden, especially if given a sunny spot with well-drained soil.

Galanthus nivalis 'Lutescens' (left), an unusual but frailer form of the common snowdrop; the large-flowered *G. elwesiii* (right) is sometimes slower to establish than *G. nivalis*

Galanthus caucasicus has noticeably grey leaves and large blooms

The common snowdrop, *Galanthus nivalis*, itself is the most widely used species for naturalizing and has a large number of forms, of which the double, with its muddled, green-flecked centre, is almost equally easily grown. 'Viridapicis' has much more green than normal on the inner segments. 'Lutescens' and 'Flavescens' are very distinct in having yellow markings instead of green, but they are less robust and do not increase so freely. 'Magnet' is unusual in carrying its flowers on very long, curving pedicels. 'Atkinsii' is a vigorous hybrid between *G. nivalis* and *G. plicatus*, some 6 in. (15 cm) or more tall.

There are several larger snowdrops, of which *Galanthus elwesii* is the commonest and one of the best garden plants. It has very broad, glaucous-grey leaves and large flowers, frequently appearing earlier than those of *G. nivalis*, but does not increase quite so readily. Other large-flowered species which are usually available are *G. byzantinus*, *G. caucasicus* and *G. plicatus*, differing a little in the greyness of the leaves, in the folding of the leaf edges and in the green markings on the segments.

All the snowdrops mentioned so far have grey-green leaves, but there are at least two which are distinct in having glossy green leaves. The most often seen are *G. ikariae* and its subspecies *latifolius*, which are easy to grow and increase well in a sunny well-drained position.

Leucojum

Leucojum is a neglected genus compared with *Galanthus*, but several snowflakes are trouble-free garden plants which deserve to be better known, while the remainder are excellent for growing under glass.

The best species for the garden are *Leucojum vernum*, flowering in the spring, *L. aestivum* in early summer and *L. autumnale* in autumn. These all do well in partial shade or in sun and present no difficulties, the first two even growing satisfactorily in grass. The spring snowflake, *L. vernum*, has glossy green leaves and stems 3 to 6 in. (8–15 cm) high, carrying one or two exquisite, cup-shaped, nodding flowers, pure white with green tips to the segments. The variety *carpathicum* differs only in having yellow tips instead of green. Flowering usually starts at the end of January or early February, whereas the summer snowflake, *L. aestivum*, flowers in late April or early May. It is a much taller plant, with stems up to 12 in. (30 cm), or even more in the clone 'Gravetye Giant'. The leaves too are longer and narrower and the flowers smaller, but with up to six on a stem.

The autumn-flowering *Leucojum autumnale* is very different, with long slender leaves and 4 in. (10 cm) reddish stems, each bearing one or two small, white, bell-shaped flowers in September

Leucojum vernum is an undemanding plant which flourishes in many different situations

The summer snowflake, *Leucojum aestivum*, does particularly well near water

and October. Its delicate appearance belies its vigour and it will soon build up into a good clump in partial shade or full sun. The rare *L. roseum* is like a miniature edition of *L. autumnale*, with pink-flushed flowers also produced in autumn. It merits cultivation under glass, as do the little spring-flowering species, *L. nicaeense*, *L. longifolium* and *L. trichophyllum*, all requiring full sun and having small white bells on 2 to 4 in. (5–10 cm) stems. Of these, *L. nicaeense* is certainly the easiest, a splendid, freely increasing pot plant.

Iris

Among the dwarf irises are some of the most exquisite spring-flowering bulbs. They fall mainly into two botanical sections of the genus, Juno and Reticulata.

RETICULATA IRISES

The Reticulata section contains many easy and beautiful plants less than 6 in. (15 cm) high, demanding only a sunny position and reasonable drainage and flowering from January to March. They usually increase by offsets, which can be detached and planted separately or left to develop into clumps. They have few troubles apart from ink disease, a serious fungal infection which can take hold in gardens where large numbers of Reticulata irises are grown. Affected bulbs have dark inky patches on them and should be destroyed; the leaves of surviving plants should be sprayed with mancozeb during the growing season. Ink disease is not common and should not deter gardeners from trying Reticulata irises.

The most widely-grown of this section is *Iris reticulata* itself, together with its various hybrids and cultivars found in bulb catalogues. The species has deep violet-blue flowers with a yellow central crest and white streaks at the base of the falls (the outer segments of the iris flower). In the variety *krelagei* the colour is a uniform reddish purple and the robust 'J. S. Dijt' is similar. 'Cantab' has a base colour of pale blue, again with a yellow crest surrounded with white. 'Clairette' is a striking form, pale blue but with a deep violet blade (the lowest portion of the fall) and a white crest with dark streaks each side of it. There are several others with deep blue flowers, which may well be hybrids with *I. histrioides*; they are exceptionally vigorous plants and increase very freely in the garden, the two best known being 'Harmony' and 'Joyce'.

The beautiful *Iris bakeriana* has pale blue flowers with a dark blue blade and conspicuous yellow crest. In the garden it enjoys the same conditions as other Reticulatas, but is less robust.

The most cheerful sight of the winter garden is the splash of colour from *Iris histrioides* 'Major', which generally opens its large, remarkably weather-resistant flowers in January. They are

'Cantab' (above) and 'Harmony' (below), two lovely and dependable
Reticulata irises

very deep blue with a yellow crest with white streaks on each side of it and they last for several weeks. A much more difficult plant, probably only suitable for cultivation under glass, is *I. histrio*, but its variety *aintabensis* is widely available and a good garden plant, with smaller, pale blue flowers.

There are two yellow-flowered Reticulata irises. Grown in vast quantity by Dutch nurserymen, *Iris danfordiae* is not a very satisfactory garden plant because, after flowering well in the first season, it then splits into small bulbils and does not flower again. Planting the bulbs at least 10 in. (25 cm) deep may discourage splitting and help to overcome this. The flower shape is unusual, with tiny standards (inner segments) and falls sloping upwards, giving a squat bunched appearance. *I. winogradowii* has only recently become obtainable in the trade and is a magnificent plant, with large yellow flowers of similar size and shape to *I. histrioides* 'Major', generally not produced until March. Although growing reasonably in sun, it seems to do better in a partially shaded position with additional humus in the soil.

Hybrids have been raised between *Iris histrioides* and *I. winogradowii*. The commonest of these are 'Katharine Hodgkin', a vigorous plant with large flowers of a curious greenish yellow streaked with blue, and 'Frank Elder' with paler flowers of a clearer blue. These usually appear in February, when the flowers of *I. histrioides* are going over.

JUNO IRISES

The Juno irises, flowering between February and April, are less widely grown because of their special requirements. Most of the smaller species are tricky and only suitable for cultivation under glass, since they need a dry period during the summer months and resent excessive moisture on their leaves at other times. This applies to the delightful yellow-flowered *I. caucasica*, which is one of the easier dwarf species, and the rarer and more difficult *I. persica*, in various greyish or yellowish shades, with deep purple or brown on the falls, and *I. nusairiensis*, with pale blue flowers.

Among the larger Juno irises are several strong-growing species which can be grown in the open garden, given a well-drained hot position, perhaps at the foot of a south-facing wall which shields them from rain in summer. One of the easiest is *Iris bucharica*, generally 1 ft (30 cm) high with lush leaves, from the axils of which arises a succession of flowers, white with yellow falls. *I. magnifica*, with white or pale blue flowers, is similar, but

Iris *winogradowii* (left), a rare species until recently but now proving very hardy; its hybrid, *I.* 'Katharine Hodgkin' (right), is also becoming more widely available

may attain up to 2 ft (60 cm) in height. Other tall species include *I. aucheri* (*I. sindjarensis*) and *I. graeberiana*, with deep blue flowers.

All these can be grown outside, at least in the south, but it is always most important to start with sound bulbs. The bulb itself is unusual in having a number of permanent thickened storage roots beneath it, which seem to be essential for it to become established and which are frequently broken off through careless handling. Propagation of Juno irises is usually by seed, although some vigorous species will increase by division.

Opposite: the aptly named *Iris magnifica* in front of a south-facing wall

Narcissus

Daffodils are among the most popular of all garden plants, although the species themselves and the smaller hybrids seem to be less appreciated than the vast array of large-flowered cultivars. Most of them are just as easily grown and have the same gift of remaining in pristine condition for several weeks during cool weather. As the foliage is less obtrusive than in their larger relations, they are more suitable for planting at the front of a border or in the rock garden and many will do well in partial shade, irrespective of how acid or alkaline the soil is. A few will grow in grass, but on the whole the larger daffodils are better for this purpose. Daffodils vary in their cultural requirements, which will be discussed below, but unless otherwise stated, it can be assumed that they will grow in any reasonable soil in an open position. (See also the Wisley Handbook, *Daffodils*.)

There are several miniatures of the typical trumpet daffodil, both species and hybrids. The smallest is *Narcissus asturiensis* (*N. minimus*), usually only 2 to 3 in. (5–8 cm) high with deep yellow flowers in proportion. Like all this group, it is easy to grow in the open garden and will tolerate a certain amount of shade. The similar but larger and later-flowering *N. minor* has stems

The diminutive *Narcissus asturiensis* comes from northern Spain, where it may be found growing in snow

Narcissus 'Hawera', a delightful Triandrus hybrid from New Zealand

generally around 6 in. (15 cm). *N. pseudonarcissus* is the wild daffodil widely distributed throughout Europe including Britain, where it is known as the Lent lily or Tenby daffodil. It has a number of named subspecies and varieties, ranging in height from 6 to 12 in. (15–30 cm) and varying in depth of colour and in the carriage of the trumpet-shaped flower, which may be horizontal or more pendulous. Two very distinct subspecies are *pallidiflorus* and *moschatus*. The first grows to about 8 in. (20 cm), with large flowers of a delicate creamy yellow. It seems to thrive in semi-shade with plenty of humus in the soil and increases slowly. The second has off-white hanging flowers and likes the same conditions.

Among the small trumpet hybrids are 'Bambi', only 6 in. (15 cm) high with creamy white petals and deep yellow trumpets, and 'W. P. Milner', which has creamy flowers on 10 in. (25 cm) stems. Other similar cultivars can be found in specialist catalogues.

The aptly named angel's tears, *Narcissus triandrus*, is an exquisite species whose pendulous flowers have long cups and recurving petals – a beautiful shape which it has imparted to its hybrids. It usually appears in catalogues as *N. triandrus* 'Albus', with creamy white flowers, and there is also a subspecies *pallidulus* (generally offered as *N. concolor*) with deep yellow flowers.

Narcissus cyclamineus, a fine species in its own right and also the parent of many outstanding hybrids

Both grow well in sun or light shade, in well-drained soil containing abundant humus.

Many of the Triandrus hybrids are a little tall to be included here, but two dwarfs with several graceful, nodding flowers to a stem are the golden 'April Tears' and pale lemon 'Hawera'.

Narcissus cyclamineus is a fine species requiring moist, preferably semi-shaded conditions, in which it may well become naturalized, increasing by division and by seed. The flower is elongated, with a long narrow trumpet and distinctive, swept back petals of similar length. It has proved a prolific parent of hybrids of all sizes, mostly with petals reflexed to some degree. The best known is probably 'Tête-à-Tête', 6 to 8 in. (15–20 cm) high with beautiful, long-lasting, deep yellow flowers, generally produced in early March and increasing very freely indeed. 'Jack Snipe' is a little taller, with a yellow cup and cream reflexed petals, and 'Beryl' has an orange cup and primrose petals. Of the larger Cyclamineus hybrids about 12 in. (30 cm) high, 'February Gold', 'February Silver', 'March Sunshine' and 'Jenny' are outstanding easy plants, the first three normally flowering in March (in spite of their names) and 'Jenny' in April.

Many species in the Jonquil group need a warm sunny position in well-drained soil; alternatively, they make excellent pot plants

The hoop-petticoat daffodil, *Narcissus bulbocodium*, seeds itself freely and will form colonies even in grass

for an unheated greenhouse or frame, benefiting from a dry period in the summer. All have fragrant flowers with small cups and petals held at right angles to them, but they differ considerably in height and in the number of flowers to a stem. *Narcissus rupicola* usually bears solitary flowers of deep yellow, as does its uncommon subspecies *marvieri*, with larger flowers. The smallest species, *N. scaberulus* and *N. gaditanus*, are only about 2 to 3 in. (5–8 cm), with several flowers on a stem. *N. assoanus* (*N. requienii*, *N. juncifolius*) is taller, up to 6 in. (15 cm), as is the more robust *N. jonquilla* itself and the slightly smaller variety *henriquesii*. A number of others are of similar height to this, 6 to 8 in. (15–20 cm), including *N. fernandesii* and *N. willkommii*.

Most members of the Tazetta group – the popular "narcissi" with clusters of scented flowers – are too large to be considered here, apart from *Narcissus canaliculatus* (*N. tazetta* subsp. *italicus*), a delightful 5 in. (12 cm) dwarf, with white petals and a yellow cup. It does best in a hot sunny spot. The hybrid, 'Minnow', is only a little taller, having cream-coloured flowers with yellow cups, and is less demanding of warmth than the species itself.

The hoop-petticoat daffodils, *Narcissus bulbocodium* and its allies, are some of the loveliest dwarf narcissus. Although varying greatly in height and colour, all have the characteristic, large,

Narcissus cantabricus var. *petunioides* is unfortunately rather scarce in cultivation

funnel-shaped cup framed with very small, unobtrusive petals. *N. bulbocodium* itself and its varieties *obesus* and *conspicuus* are among the most vigorous and grow well in the open garden or even in grass, as at the RHS Garden at Wisley where they are a wonderful sight in early spring. These usually have deep yellow flowers, while the equally vigorous var. *citrinus* is pale primrose. The smallest variety is the very early-flowering *nivalis*, some 3 in. (8 cm) high, which is probably best with glass protection. *N. romieuxii* also flowers extremely early, in January or even before, and is often recommended for cultivation under glass, but does well in the open in a sunny well-drained position and increases readily. The flowers are pale yellow with protuberant stamens.

The species *Narcissus cantabricus* and its relatives are very similar to *N. bulbocodium*, with white flowers, and originate from southern Spain and North Africa. They are dwarf, early and very beautiful, but do best under glass with a summer drying-off period. The finest of all is *N. cantabricus* var. *petunioides*, in which the cup is flared out to the horizontal – a most unusual shape. 'Julia Jane' resembles it, but in pale yellow.

Tulipa

The large hybrid tulips, which have been developed so magnificently over the centuries by Dutch growers, now bear little resemblance to the wild species and it is among the latter that almost all the dwarf tulips are found. To many gardeners, tulips seem too formal for anything but bedding and they rarely make good garden plants if left alone in a permanent position like daffodils. However, whereas the dwarf narcissus species are usually a little more difficult to grow than the hybrids, the reverse seems to be the case with tulips and there are many delightful species under 12 in. (30 cm) in height which persist and increase when planted in the open garden.

With only one exception, tulips need an open sunny site and a well-drained soil. The rock garden or a raised bed are therefore ideal positions for the smaller ones and the front of a sunny border for the larger. Some species are reluctant to increase by division and can only be propagated by seed, which takes from four to six years to attain flowering size.

The tulips described here are generally available from nurserymen and make satisfactory garden plants, at least in the south of England. Some of the rarer species occasionally offered do better under glass, where they can be given the summer drying-off period which they receive in nature, and this treatment will suit any of the species in colder areas. They offer a wide range of colours, from white and yellow through pink to purple and shades of scarlet, frequently with a contrasting colour on the outside of the petals. The main flowering time is April.

Tulipa biflora is a small species roughly 4 in. (10 cm) high, with up to three flowers to a stem, white with yellow at the base and tinged grey on the outside. Of somewhat similar colouring are *T. polychroma* and *T. turkestanica*, the latter with conspicuous brown anthers.

The lady tulip, *Tulipa clusiana*, is one of the most beautiful of all, about 6 to 8 in. (15–20 cm) high, with a starry white flower stained deep rose on the outside. The variety *chrysantha* (*T. chrysantha*) differs only in having a yellow base colour. Another easily grown species of similar size is *T. tarda* (*T. dasystemon*); the white flowers in April and May have at least the inner third of each petal yellow and greenish shading on the reverse.

The only tulip flourishing in shady conditions is *Tulipa*

sylvestris, naturalized in parts of England. It is an easy garden plant which increases freely when planted among shrubs, although it is sometimes shy to flower. The flowers are yellow with green outside and tend, in shade, to have outward-curving stems. A first-class rock garden plant some 4 to 6 in. (10–15 cm) high, *Tulipa urumiensis* has large, short-stemmed, yellow flowers streaked externally with bronze. *T. batalinii* is another very good large-flowered dwarf, the colour a soft creamy yellow. It is probably a subspecies of the red *T. linifolia* (p.42).

Pinks and purples are represented in the highly variable species, *Tulipa humilis*, under which are included *T. pulchella*, *T. violacea* and *T. aucheriana*. The colour of *T. humilis* in the wild ranges from light pink to deep purple, usually with a central yellow blotch. In cultivation, the paler colours are generally seen in *T. humilis* and *T. pulchella*, the darker in *T. violacea*. A delightful, easily grown dwarf *T. aucheriana*, is only 3 to 4 in. (8–10 cm) high, with pink flowers with a yellow centre. The rare *T. violacea* var. *pallida* is particularly striking, white with a deep violet blotch. All are very early flowering, in February and March, but can be grown in the open.

Tulipa saxatilis and the very similar *T. bakeri* flower later, normally in April, and have glossy green leaves and 8 in. (20 cm) stems bearing one to three large pink flowers. The bulbs are stoloniferous and rapidly form a large colony, which unfortunately does not flower freely until well established. In this respect, *T. bakeri* seems to be a more satisfactory plant than *T. saxatilis*. *T. cretica* is an excellent miniature of these, which will survive average winters in the open in the warmer countries, and makes an excellent pot plant.

Many of the red-flowered species are slightly large to be considered dwarf bulbs, but nevertheless are good garden plants, for example, *Tulipa eichleri*, *T. fosteriana*, *T. praestans*, *T. greigii* and the magnificent *T. sprengeri*, which is easily grown and one of the latest to flower, often at the end of May. Much smaller at about 12 in. (30 cm) are *T. hageri*, *T. orphanidea* and *T. whittallii*, whose reddish flowers are heavily marked with bronze or green and consequently less vivid than the pure reds. Among dwarf pure red species are *T. maximowiczii* and *T. linifolia*, which are excellent

Opposite, top: *Tulipa biflora* (left) and *T. turkestanica* (right), two vigorous dwarf tulips

Centre: *T. urumiensis* (left) and *T. batalinii* (right) can be recommended for the rock garden

Bottom: *T. bakeri* (left) and *T. sprengeri* (right) flower at the end of the tulip season

The compact *Tulipa kaufmanniana* produces its large flowers early in the year

plants for the rock garden. Attractive hybrids between *T. linifolia* and the yellow *T. batalinii* are available in shades of creamy bronze or apricot, such as 'Bronze Charm'.

Tulipa greigii is the parent of a large number of spectacular hybrids, often with striped leaves, flowering in March. Some of the best small varieties are 'Ali Baba', pale pink with scarlet interior, 'Donna Bella', pale yellow with a dark base and red exterior, 'Dreamboat', salmon, 'Ontario', pink, 'Plaisir', yellow streaked with red, and 'Red Riding Hood', scarlet.

T. fosteriana has also produced several good hybrids, usually flowering in April, though somewhat tall to be mentioned here at up to 18 in. (45 cm). They include 'Madam Lefeber', bright red, 'Candela', yellow, 'Orange Emperor', orange, and 'Purissima', white.

The hybrids of the waterlily tulip, *T. kaufmanniana*, are splendid garden plants, with flowers which open wide in the sun, on stems of only 6 to 8 in. (15–20 cm), often produced as early as February. In a reasonably well-drained soil, they will persist and even increase better than most other hybrid tulips. The species itself has pale yellow flowers streaked outside with red and is one of the most reliable. Some of the best of the large range of hybrids are 'Alfred Cortot', red, 'Cesar Frank' and 'Gluck', red with yellow inside, 'Chopin' and 'Berlioz', yellow, 'Johann Strauss' and 'The First', white with some red on the reverse, and 'Fritz Kreisler' and 'Heart's Delight', in mixed shades of pink, yellow and red.

Dwarf Bulbs for Autumn and Winter

SEPTEMBER TO NOVEMBER

Some of the autumn-flowering bulbs have already been described in the chapters on crocus, colchicum, galanthus and leucojum. There are in addition several species of cyclamen, sternbergia and zephyranthes which can be relied upon to flower in the garden at this season.

Many of the hardy cyclamen are easy to grow and can become an increasingly attractive feature of the garden as they multiply from self-sown seed. This applies especially to the autumn-flowering *Cyclamen hederifolium* (*C. neapolitanum*) and the later *C. coum*, which should be planted with their corms just below the surface of the soil in the shade of trees or shrubs and are quite trouble-free. It is always advisable to start with actively growing corms in pots or packed in peat, rather than the cheaper dried corms which may never establish. The soil should be well drained with extra humus incorporated in the form of peat or, better still, leaf mould, which is relished by all cyclamen.

The popular *Cyclamen hederifolium* has pink flowers and attractive dark green leaves with silver patterns; there is also an excellent white variety. Of the other species, *C. cilicium*, with smaller, pale pink flowers, and the related tiny-flowered *C. intaminatum* are hardy in the south at least. So too is *C. mirabile*, which is similar to *C. cilicium*, except that the leaves have a more obvious purple flush and toothed edges. *C. purpurascens* (still better known as *C. europaeum*) has scented pink flowers and is widely available, but lacks the vigour of the other hardy species. It seems to benefit from deep planting.

The remaining autumn-flowering cyclamen are slightly tender and make fine plants for the cold greenhouse, given a well-drained compost (as described on p.13), preferably with the addition of sieved leaf mould. *Cyclamen graecum* has beautifully marbled leaves and pale to deep pink flowers, but does not always produce these freely, even with the summer baking which it seems to need more than most species. *C. africanum* resembles a large-leaved *C. hederifolium* and *C. cyprium* has small, white, scented flowers with a pink spot at the base. The uncommon *C. rohlfsianum* bears fragrant, deep crimson flowers in autumn, but is more tender and more difficult to grow.

Sternbergia lutea looks like a deep yellow crocus, about 6 in. (15 cm) high with glossy green leaves appearing with the flowers

Above: the white-flowered variety of the popular and easily grown *Cyclamen hederifolium*

Below: *Sternbergia lutea* makes a charming contribution to the autumn garden

in September and October. It has a reputation for being shy-flowering, although different clones seem to vary in this respect. Plant it in the hottest position possible and leave well alone; the number of flowers should then increase from year to year. The variety *angustifolia* (*S. sicula*) has narrower leaves and is said to be freer-flowering.

Zephyranthes candida is the only hardy member of the genus which is readily available in Britain. It has small crocus-like flowers on 6 in. (15 cm) stems, accompanying long narrow leaves. The flowers are white with a greenish flush at the base.

DECEMBER TO FEBRUARY

Every gardener likes to see a few flowers outside during the winter months and dwarf bulbs can be depended on to produce them, except when there is snow on the ground. Many autumn-flowering bulbs, especially crocuses and cyclamen, will continue to flower sparsely until Christmas and, in a mild season, spring-flowering bulbs such as snowdrops, crocuses and Reticulata irises will be starting before the end of February. There are a number of other dwarf bulbs which will flower in the winter months, particularly January and February, if the weather is not exceptionally harsh.

The winter aconites are well named, their leaves and yellow flowers appearing amazingly quickly with the first spell of good weather in January to make a carpet among shrubs, dividing and self-sowing freely once they are established. *Eranthis hyemalis*, the commonest species, has clear yellow, upturned flowers sur-rounded with a ruff of narrow leaves. The taller *E.* 'Guinea Gold' has larger flowers and bronzy leaves.

Eranthis 'Guinea Gold' is taller than some other *Eranthis*

Above: a carpet of colours provided by the vigorous *Cyclamen coum*

Below: *Anemone blanda* (left) and its forms, such as 'White Splendour' (right), flower as early as February

The intense blue of *Scilla sibirica* (left) is always welcome in spring;
S. tubergeniana (right) is more restrained, but an enchanging plant

Cyclamen coum has the same vigour and favours the same conditions as *C. hederifolium* (p.43). It generally begins flowering in January and is an immensely variable plant, with numerous related species and subspecies ranging in colour from white to the deepest magenta and having plain or marbled leaves. If several of these are planted together, they will sow themselves around and a galaxy of colours and leaf forms will eventually appear.

The first of the anemones to flower is *Anemone blanda*, a beautiful, easily grown species, especially in partial shade in a limy soil, with deep lavender-blue flowers. There are several excellent named forms offered by nurserymen, among them the much darker 'Atrocaerulea', 'White Splendour' and the pink 'Rosea'. 'Radar' is unusual, being deep magenta-pink with a broad white centre. All these increase gradually from the tubers in rich soil and also seed themselves, flowering after a year or two in a variety of colours, including wishy-washy intermediates unless the named forms are kept well apart.

The earliest of the scillas usually flower in February and make a real impact in the garden with their brilliant blue colour, flourishing and seeding themselves in sun, or in partial shade, where they contrast with snowdrops and aconites. The two best are *Scilla sibirica*, which is usually sold as a selected clone, 'Spring Beauty', with several deep blue flowers on a 3 to 4 in. (8–10 cm) stem, and *S. bifolia* of similar size but with smaller flowers of not quite such a vivid colour. The third common scilla flowering in February is *S. tubergeniana*, which has white flowers with a blue stripe down the centre of each petal.

Dwarf Bulbs for Spring

As well as the familiar spring-flowering bulbs – narcissus, crocus, iris and tulip – there are many other bulbs belonging to smaller genera which flower at this time, from March to mid-May.

SHADE-LOVERS

Some spring-flowering bulbs, unlike most bulbous plants, need a moist humus-rich soil in semi-shade to thrive. Trillium and erythronium are the most important of these and anemone, fritillaria and cyclamen also contribute several shade-loving species.

Given suitable conditions, the majority of trilliums are easy to grow and once established will form gradually increasing clumps. Those which are widely available are exquisite plants with large three-lobed leaves and three-petalled flowers. The commonest is the wake robin, *Trillium grandiflorum*, which carries sumptuous white flowers well above the leaves in April, growing 8 in. (20 cm) or more in height. A double form, like a formal double camellia in flower shape, can sometimes be obtained and there is also a wonderful pink variety occasionally seen. The slightly smaller *T. ovatum* resembles *T. grandiflorum* and is an equally good, easy garden plant in shade. The flowers are usually smaller and the petals narrower with less overlap.

The interesting *Trillium sessile* has chocolate-brown flowers which are upright and sessile (stalkless) on the broad marbled leaves, while *T. luteum* has greenish yellow flowers. In *T. erectum*,

Trillium grandiflorum (left), with glistening white blooms, and its highly desirable pink variety (right)

The curious, upright, dark-coloured flowers of *Trillium sessile*

on the other hand, the flowers are carried on long curved stalks, so that they are horizontal or even nodding. The colour is usually reddish brown and there is also an excellent white variety with a dark centre.

Occasionally offered but unfortunately more difficult to grow, *Trillium undulatum* is similar to *T. erectum* and has generally smaller flowers beautifully striped with dark red. It is about 6 to 9 in. (15–22 cm) high. The much smaller *T. nivale* is only 1 to 2 in. (2–5 cm) high with small white flowers, in some forms heavily speckled with pink. *T. nivale* resembles it, but always has white flowers. Neither are particularly difficult to grow outside and they also make fine pot plants under glass.

Shade-loving plants often seem to have a special delicacy and grace and of no genus is this truer than the erythroniums, curiously named dog's tooth violets: the tubers have some resemblance to dogs' teeth and the flowers remarkably little resemblance to violets! All have exquisite nodding flowers with recurving petals, in a range of colours and with the leaves variously marked or plain. They may be propagated by division or from seed. *Erythronium dens-canis*, from which the common name originates, is certainly the most frequently advertised in nursery catalogues, but is not the best garden plant in most areas, for it often fails to flower well. However, the blotching or mottling of the leaves can be very striking and the flowers are a good pink, with yellow-brown at the base of the petals and dark anthers. It is about 5 in. (12 cm) high. The most satisfactory of the pink-flowered species is the very robust *E. revolutum*, which has distinctly-marked leaves and pale to deep pink flowers with yellow anthers, increasing well in peaty soil. The less vigorous *E. hendersonii* has pinkish lavender flowers with a dark centre.

Of the yellow species, *Erythronium tuolumnense* is one of the best and easiest to grow, with pale green, glossy leaves and one to three deep yellow flowers to a stem. The hybrids, 'Pagoda', 'Kondo' and 'Jeannine' are taller, with slightly larger flowers. *E. americanum* is a very dwarf, yellow species with lovely mottled leaves compensating for its rather shy flowering habit.

Several erythroniums have creamy white flowers, usually with deeper yellow at the base of the petals. Of these, *Erythronium oregonum*, *E. californicum* and *E. helenae* are very similar, up to 8 in. (20 cm) tall, beautiful and easy to grow. The most vigorous of all is 'White Beauty', which may be derived from *E. oregonum*.

Most anemones thrive in woodland conditions, including the winter-flowering *Anemone blanda* (p.47). Our native wood anemone, *A. nemorosa*, in its better selected forms, is ideal for growing among shrubs and will contend with deep shade. Many named forms can be found in specialist catalogues; some of the best are the double white 'Alboplena', the larger pale blue 'Robinsoniana' and 'Allenii' and the darker 'Royal Blue'. 'Leeds' Variety' is an exceptionally large-flowered, single white and there are one or two named pink forms.

Anemone apennina is very similar to *A. blanda* with its large, semi-double, pale blue or white flowers, but is more suitable for dense shade, where it will increase well, the seedlings remaining true to colour since there is little variation in this species. In the same situation, *A. ranunculoides* can provide a contrast with small, deep yellow flowers, spreading very freely in peaty soil. There are double forms of it and also a hybrid with *A. nemorosa* – the beautiful pale yellow *A. × lipsiensis*. These anemones generally grow to about 6 in. (15 cm) high.

Cyclamen coum (p.47) starts flowering very early and continues well into the spring, to be followed by *C. repandum*, another shade-loving species with marbled leaves and deep magenta flowers. Recently, a form from southern Greece, ssp. *peloponnesiacum*, has become more generally available, with paler pink flowers and leaves strikingly spotted with white. *C. repandum* is a little less hardy than *C. coum* and this probably applies especially to ssp. *peloponnesiacum*. *C. libanoticum* has

Above: *Erythronium revolutum* (left) and E. 'White Beauty' (right) are two robust dog's tooth violets

Below: 'Robinsoniana' is an excellent form of the wood anemone, A. *nemorosa*

Above: a mixture of the blue *Anemone apennina* and its white form
Below: the double form of *A. ranunculoides* (left); *Fritillaria camschat-censis* (right) is one of the species which prefers shade

the largest, pale pink flowers of all the species. It has acquired an unfortunate reputation for needing cold greenhouse treatment, whereas in fact it can withstand temperatures lower than 0°F (−18°C). It too does best in partial shade.

Although the majority of fritillaries require hot dry conditions, there are some which need shade, humus and moisture to thrive. Into this category fall the uncommon Himalayan species, *Fritillaria cirrhosa*, which has large flowers, either slightly chequered yellow or heavily chequered almost brown, on 8 in. (20 cm) stems, and *F. camschatcensis*, an intriguing plant native to eastern Asia, Alaska and Canada, with nearly black flowers. Another American species and a woodland native is the very variable *F. lanceolata*, up to 18 in. (45 cm) high with several small, dark-spotted flowers to a stem.

SUN-LOVERS

Most fritillaries enjoy a well-drained soil in full sun and the recent introduction or reintroduction of many species has created tremendous interest in the genus. They display an amazing diversity of shape and size and, although their bell-shaped flowers are frequently in sombre shades of green and brown, there are many with brighter colouring. In this limited space, only those which can be easily grown in the open garden are described, but many rarer species are now available from specialists and present little difficulty in a cold greenhouse or frame. Seed is the ideal method of propagation, but many increase by division or by forming small bulbils.

The native snakeshead, *Fritillaria meleagris*, is the most popular, with beautifully chequered bells in pinkish purple or white; it is easily grown in sun or partial shade and even flourishes in grass. In sunny gardens, *F. pyrenaica* is the most reliable of all, with robust 12 in. (30 cm) stems and flowers which are generally deep chocolate in colour, but may vary from pale greenish yellow through intermediate shades. *F. persica* is very different in appearance, with rosettes of grey-green leaves from which emerge tall spikes of small flowers. These may attain as much as 2½ ft (75 cm) in the robust clone 'Adiyaman', which has deep purple flowers with a grape-like bloom, and forms with pale greenish flowers also occur. This species needs a very sunny place to flower well. *F. montana* (*F. nigra*) and the very closely allied *F. ruthenica* grow up to 12 to 18 in. (30–45 cm) high and have several small, very dark brown chequered flowers to a stem.

The Japanese *Fritillaria verticillata*, bearing 2 ft (60 cm) spikes of small straw-coloured flowers, may take a year or two to

Above: *Fritillaria pyrenaica* (left), easily grown in a sunny spot, and *F. pallidiflora* (right), which is better with a little shade

Below: the large, strikingly coloured bells of *F. michailovskyi* (left); the smaller-flowered *F. uva-vulpis* (right) increases freely

become established and flower well, but tolerates cooler conditions. Two other large-flowered species which prefer some shade are *F. raddeana* and *F. pallidiflora*. The former is like a small version of the crown imperial, *F. imperialis*, with flowers of a beautiful greeny yellow. *F. pallidiflora* is an excellent garden plant, easily raised from seed, with rounded glaucous leaves and unusually large, pale yellow flowers, up to three to a stem.

There are many smaller fritillaries suitable for the rock garden or the front of a well-drained border. One of the most exciting recent introductions from Turkey is *Fritillaria michailovskyi*, only 3 to 4 in. (8–10 cm) high with comparatively large flowers, which are deep chocolate towards the base and bright yellow over the outer third – a spectacular contrast. The same colour contrast is seen in *F. uva-vulpis* (*F. assyriaca*), with much smaller flowers on slightly taller stems. *F. minuta* (*F. carduchorum*) is very distinctive in having abundant glossy green leaves and small brick-red flowers.

There are several fritillaries some 6 to 8 in. (15–25 cm) high which have greenish flowers, either plain or faintly chequered or shaded. Among them are *Fritillaria involucrata*, the very easily grown *F. pontica*, *F. graeca* subsp. *thessala*, also a good garden plant, the taller *F. messanensis* in various forms and the slightly less robust *F. hermonis* subsp. *amana*.

The genus *Corydalis* contains some excellent sun-loving species, with characteristic, tubular, two-lipped flowers and much-divided foliage. *Corydalis solida* is very easy, increasing freely from the tubers and from seed, and has attractive greyish, ferny leaves and 4 in. (10 cm) spikes of purple flowers. *C. decipiens* and the variety *densiflora* (*C. densiflora*) are almost identical to it. *C. solida* 'George Baker' is a magnificent form (originally introduced under the incorrect name of *C. transsilvanica*), with flowers of an exquisite shade of pinkish terracotta. Although rare, it is hardy and very easy to grow in the garden. *C. caucasica* var. *alba* has pure white flowers and seeds itself around in sun or partial shade. *C. bulbosa* (*C. cava*) is a more robust plant which again increases readily, with purple or white flowers.

The flowering of the chionodoxas, known as glory of the snow, usually overlaps with that of the scillas (p.47) and indeed the two are closely related and frequently hybridize. Chionodoxas are mostly of similar height, up to 6 in. (15 cm), but differ from *Scilla bifolia* and *S. sibirica* in having more white in the flowers. The commonest species is *C. luciliae*, sometimes offered as the larger *C. gigantea*, which has blue flowers with a clear white centre, except in the pale pink form, 'Rosea'. It increases rapidly both by division and self-seeding. *C. sardensis* is similar but smaller, while

'George Baker' a superb form of *Corydalis solida*, which is hardy and easily cultivated

the Cretan *C. nana*, only 2 to 4 in. (5–10 cm) high, is the smallest and most delicate of all.

Puschkinia scilloides is very similar to chionodoxa. It is an excellent garden plant whose white flowers have a conspicuous blue line down the centre of the petals. There is also a beautiful pure white variety.

The grape hyacinths are well-known to every gardener, with their spikes of tightly packed bells with incurving lips, ranging from white, through shades of blue, to an unusual deep, almost black colour. All are easily grown; indeed several can become a nuisance, forming myriads of small bulbils which are spread around by digging, and these are only suitable for wilder parts of the garden. Names to beware of in this respect are *Muscari racemosum* and *M. neglectum*, probably synonymous and referring to plants with dense, dark blue, white-rimmed flowers.

Of the many species, varying only in colour, *Muscari azureum*, with clear blue flowers, darker towards the base of the spike, and *M. armenaicum*, with pale blue white-tipped flowers, are the most frequently offered. The tassel hyacinth, *M. comosum*, is much taller, up to 12 in. (30 cm), and has scattered straw-coloured flowers at the base of the spike with densely packed, dark purple flowers above, surmounted by a tassel of paler mauve flowers.

Above: *Corydalis caucascia* (left) delights in sun or some shade;
'Rosea' (right) a pink form of the versatile *Chionodoxa gigantea*

Below: *Puschkinia scilloides* (left), flowers in very early spring; the odd
feather-duster blooms of *Muscari comosum* 'Plumosum' (right)

Ornithogalum nutans (left) is suitable for naturalizing among shrubs;
'Wisley Blue' (right), an attractive darker form of *Ipheion uniflorum*

This is very easy to grow, but not to everyone's taste. A form known as 'Plumosum' or 'Monstrosum' is sometimes offered, in which all the flowers consist of elongated mauvish tassels.

The genus *Ornithogalum* contains a large number of dwarf species, usually very low-growing and having heads of white flowers with some green markings, but few are in general cultivation. The commonest is *Ornithogalum umbellatum*, the star of Bethlehem, one of the taller species with 6 to 8 in. (15–20 cm) stems bearing several starry white flowers and easily grown in sun or partial shade. *O. nutans* is similar in height, but the large flowers have an intriguing silvery appearance with a grey green backing to the petals. When established, it increases very freely and is perhaps best among shrubs rather than among more delicate plants. The numerous smaller species are all easy to grow in well-drained soil in full sun.

Ipheion uniflorum (*Triteleia uniflora*) is an undemanding plant which thrives in most soils. It has a cluster of narrow leaves and 6 in. (15 cm) stems, each carrying a large, very pale lavender flower with a deeper line down the centre of the petals. 'Wisley Blue' has flowers of a much deeper blue and the recently available 'Froyle Mill' produces even darker flowers, but possibly has a less robust constitution.

Dwarf Bulbs for Summer

By early May, the main flush of bulbs is over, although a few late flowers may still be seen, especially on the tulips, with the brilliant T. *sprengeri* (p. 40) still to come as an afterthought. There are, however, several dwarf bulbs which flower in the summer months, from May to August. Some of them are easily grown plants, while others are on the borderline of hardiness, but worth trying outside in the southern counties.

The alliums or onions contribute a number of hardy bulbous species flowering at some time during the summer. All have globular umbels of flowers, arranged like umbrella spokes, and most smell of onions when crushed. Many excellent plants are too tall to mention here, but *Allium pulchellum* can just be considered, with stems 8 to 10 in. (20–25 cm) high, having rounded heads of pink or white flowers, the lower pendant and the upper upright. Very easy and seeding itself freely, this is one of the best onions to grow in sun or light shade. The similar A. *flavum* is generally a little smaller, with yellow flowers, and varies considerably, the shortest forms, about 4 to 6 in. (10–15 cm) high, being classed as 'Nanum', 'Pumilum' or 'Minus'. In the best varieties, the stems have a noticeable grey bloom which enhances their beauty. The dependable A. *moly* has broad heads of larger yellow flowers on

The dwarf form of the variable *Allium flavum* is a useful plant for the rock garden

Above: *Triteleia laxa* (left) is very hardy and reliable; *T. ixioides* (right) should succeed in a warm position

Below: *Anomatheca laxa* (left) is the only species which can be tried outside; 'Dawn' (right) a form of the tiny *Rhodohypoxis baurii*, provides a long succession of pink flowers

8 in. (20 cm) stems, but makes bulbils excessively and should only be used where it can naturalize unhindered.

One of the best blue-flowered species, *Allium caeruleum* is small enough to be suitable for the rock garden. Most of the smaller species, up to some 10 in. (25 cm) high, have flowers in shades of pink or lavender, among the finest being *A. acuminatum*, and *A. murrayanum*, the latter probably a larger-flowered version of *A. unifolium*. Although the leaves of alliums are often narrow and inconspicuous, in two species they are an important feature. *A. karataviense* has very broad purple-backed leaves and large round heads of pinkish flowers. It is easily grown and worth planting for the leaves alone. *A. akaka* has slightly smaller leaves without the purple tinge, but the large flowerheads are usually a better pink or greenish white colour. It needs a warm position.

Brodiaea and *Triteleia* are two closely related American genera, producing allium-like flowers from late spring to early summer. Many brodiaeas, as they are usually called in nursery lists, belong correctly to *Triteleia*. Although not widely grown, some species are easy and relatively hardy and are useful for contributing shades of blue among shrubs, where that colour is often lacking. *Triteleia laxa* (*Brodiaea laxa*) is an excellent garden plant which has proved hardy down to 0°F (−18°C) and which increases and seeds itself freely. It has loose umbels of pale lavender flowers on stems up to 12 in. (30 cm) high. *B. elegans* and *T. bridgesii* (*B. bridgesii*) are lower-growing, with flowers of a good deep colour.

In addition to these and several other blue-flowered species offered occasionally under *Brodiaea* or *Triteleia*, there are two fine yellow-flowered plants – *Triteleia ixioides* (*Brodiaea lutea*) and *T. crocea* (*B. crocea*), Both have loose heads of yellow flowers, usually with a dark stripe down the centre of each petal, and are hardy in a sunny sheltered place.

Zigadenus is another American genus not often seen in gardens. Two bulbous species sometimes available are *Zigadenus fremontii* and *Z. micranthus*. The leaves appear early in the autumn, but flowering does not usually start until the end of April or later. The flower spikes, 6 to 8 in. (15–20 cm) high, carry a dozen or more small, pale yellow flowers with greenish centres, considerably larger in *Z. fremontii*. They are hardy, at least in the south.

The most spectacular American bulbs are in the genus *Calochortus*, but they are only obtainable from a few specialists and most need to be grown in a greenhouse or frame. The two species most likely to succeed in a warm well-drained position in

'Albrighton', another beautiful selection of Rhodohypoxis *baurii*

the garden are *Calochortus uniflorus* (*C. lilacinus*), with cup-shaped lilac flowers, and *C. venustus*, generally having large, creamy white or yellow flowers with a dark red central blotch.

Habranthus tubispathus (*H. andersonii, Zephyranthes andersonii*) from South America is extremely easy under glass and will survive all but the hardest winters outside. It has bright orange flowers streaked with brown on the outside of the petals, resembling a miniature hippeastrum, to which *Habranthus* are closely allied. These are usually produced in June or July. It seeds itself freely.

Flowering at the same time, the African *Anomatheca laxa* (*Lapeirousia cruenta*) is equally easy in a cool greenhouse and hardy enough to be grown outside in the south. The 6 to 8 in. (15–20 cm) slender stems bear several small, reddish pink flowers with deep red markings towards the base. It sets abundant bright red seeds and sows itself readily under glass. The variety *albus* has pure white flowers.

The South African *Rhodohypoxis* are also hardy in sheltered gardens, but they require a more peaty soil and should not be allowed to dry out completely. They are fascinating plants, ideal for a trough or rock garden, or for pots under glass, since they grow only 2 in. (5 cm) high or less and produce plentiful flowers in shades of pink, red or white, during May and June.

The first species to be introduced was *Rhodohypoxis baurii*, with red or pink flowers, together with the white or very pale variety *platypetala*. From these a number of selections have been made, such as 'Great Scot' and 'Douglas', red, 'Dawn', 'Stella' and 'Fred Broome', pink, and 'Ruth', white. The largest flowered vigorous selections now available are 'Tetra Red', 'Tetra Pink' and 'Tetra White'. The hardy and freely increasing *R. milloides* is occasionally available and has deep magenta flowers.

Zephyranthes candida is a hardy species which flowers in autumn and can be grown outside in well-drained soil

Index

Figures in **bold** refer to illustrations.

Allium acuminatum 61; A. akaka 61; A. caeruleum 61; A. flavum & forms 59, **59**; A. karataviense 61; A. × lipsiensis 50; A. moly 59–61; A. murrayanum **6**, 61; A. pulchellum 59
Anemone apennina 50, **52**; A. blanda & forms **46**, 47; A. nemorosa & forms 50, **51**; A. ranunculoides 50, **52**; A. × seemanii 50
Anomatheca laxa (Lapeirousia cruenta) & var. albus **60**, 62

Brodiaea elegans 61

Calochorius uniflorus (C. lilacinus) 61–2; C. venustus **14**, 61–2
Chionodoxa gigantea & 'Rosea' 55, **57**; C. luciliae 55; C. nana 56; C. sardensis 55
Colchicum agrippinum **1**, 24; C. atropurpureum 23; C. autumnale & forms 23; C. bivonae (C. bowlesianum) 24; C. boissieri 24; C. cilicium23; C. cupanii 24; C. hungaricum 24; C. luteum 24; C. macrophyllum 23; C. sibthorpii 24; C. speciosum & 'Album' 23, **24**
Corydalis bulbosa (C. cava) **55**; C. caucasica var. alba 55, **57**; C. decipiens & var. densiflora (C. densiflora) **55**; C. solida & 'George Baker' 55, **58**
Crocus ancyrensis 20, **21**; C. asturicus 'Atropurpureus' 19–20; C. banaticus (C. iridiflorus) 19; C. biflorus subspp. alexandri, biflorus, weldenii **21**, 22; C. cartwrightianus 19; C. crysanthus & hybrids **14**, 22; C. corsicus 22; C. dalmaticus 22; C. flavus (C. aureus) 21–2; C. fleischeri 20, **21**; C. goulimyl 20; C. hadriaticus **20**; C. 'Hubert Edelsten' **21**, 22; C. imperati 20; C. kotschyanus (C. zonatus) & var. leucopharynx (C. karduchorum) 19, **21**; C. laevigatus & 'Fontenayi' 20; C. medius 19; C. minimus 22; C. nudiflorus 19; C. ochroleucus 20; C. olivieri & subsp. balansae 22; C. pulchellus & 'Zephyr' 19; C. sativus 19; C. serotinus subsp. salzmanii 19; C. sieberi & var. tricolor 22; C. speciosus & cvs 19, **21**; C. tommasinianus & cvs **22**, **back cover**; C. vernus 22
Cyclamen africanum 43; C. cilicium 43; C. coum **14**, 43, **46**, 47; C. cyprium 43; C. graecum 43; C. hederifolium (C. neopolitanum), 43, **44**; C. intaminatum 43; C. libanoticum 50–53; C. mirabile 43; C. purpurascens (C. europaeum) 43; C. repandum & ssp. peloponnesiacum 50; C. rohlfsianum 43

Eranthis 'Guinea Gold' 45–7, **45**; E. hyemalis **14**, 45–7
Erythronium americanum 50; E. californicum 50; E. dens-canis 49–50; E. helenae 50; E. hendersonii 50; E. oregonum **2**, 50; E. revolutum 50, **51**; E. tuolumnense & 'Jeannie', 'Kondo' and 'Pagoda' 50; E. 'White Beauty 50, **51**

Fritillaria camschatcensis **52**, 53; F. cirrhosa 53; F. gracca subsp. thessala 55; F. hermonis subsp. amana 55; F. involucrata 55; F. lanceolata 50; F. meleagris **8**, 53; F. messanensis 55; F. michallovskyi **54**, 55; F. minuta (F. carduchorum) 55; F. montana (F. nigra) 53; F. pallidiflora **54**, 55; F. persica & 'Adiyaman' 53; F. pontica 55; F. pyrenaica 53, **54**; F. raddeana 55; F. ruthenica 53; F. uva-vulpis (F. assyriaca) **54**, 55; F. verticillata 53–5

Calanthus 'Atkinsii' 26; G. byzantinus 26; G. caucasicus 26, **26**; G. elwesii **25**, 26; G. ikariae & subsp. latifolius 26; G. nivalis & forms **25**, 26;

subsp. reginae-olgae (G. corcyrensis, G. reginae-olgae) 25–6; G. plicatus 26

Habranthus tubispathus (H. andersonii, Zephyranthes andersonii) 62

Ipheion uniflorum (Tritelia uniflora) & cvs 58, **58**
Iris aucheri (I. sindjarensis) **32**; I. bakeriana 29; I. bucharica 31; I. caucasica 31; I. danfordiae 31; I. 'Frank Elder' 31; I. graeberiana 32; I. 'Harmony' 29, **30**; I. histrio 30; var. aintabensis 31; I. histrioides 'Major' **16**, 29–31; I. 'Joyce' 29; I. 'Katharine Hodgkin', 31, **32**; I. magnifica 31–2, **33**; I. nusairiensis 31; I. persica 31; I. reticulata & cvs **front cover**, 29, **30**; var. krelagei 29; I. winogradowii 31, **32**

Leucojum aestivum & 'Gravetye Giant' 27, **28**; L. autumnale 27–28; L. longifolium 28; L. nicanense 28; L. roseum 28; L. trichophyllum 28; L. vernum & var. carpathicum 27, **27**

Muscari armeniacum 56; M. azureum 56; M. comosum 56; 'Plumosum' **57**, 58

Narcissus assoanus (N. requienii, N. juncifolius) 37; N. asturiensis (N. minimus) 34, **34**; N. 'Bambi' 35; N. bulbacodium & vars 37–8, **37**; N. canaliculatus (N. tazetta subsp. italicus) **37**; N. cantabricus & var. petunioides 38, **38**; N. cyclamineus & hybrids 36, **36**; N. fernandesii **37**; N. gaditanus 37; N. jonquilla & var. henriquesii **37**; N. 'Julia Jane' 38; N. minor 34–5; N. 'Minnow' 37; N. pseudonarcissus & subspp. 35; N. romieuxii 38; N. rupicola & subsp. marvieri 37; N. scaberulus 37; N. triandrus & hybrids 35–6, **35**; subsp. pallidulus (N. concolor) 35–6; N. wilkommii 37; N. 'W. P. Milner' 35

Ornithogalum nutans 58, **58**; O. umbellatum 58

Puschkinia scilloides 56, **57**

Rhodohypoxis baurii & cvs **60**, **62**; var. platypetala 62; R. milloides 62

Scilla bifolia 47; S. sibirica ('Spring Beauty') 47, **47**; S. tubergeniana 47, **47**
Sternbergia lutea 43–5, **44**; var. angustifolia (S. sicula) 45

Trillium erectum 48; T. grandiflorum 48, **48**; T. luteum 48; T. nivale 49; T. ovatum 48; T. rivale 49; T. sessile 48, 49; T. undulatum 49
Triteleia bridgesii (Brodiaea bridgesii) 61; T. crocea (B. crocea) 61; T. ixioides (B. lutea) **60**, 61; T. laxa (B. laxa) **60**, 61
Tulipa aucheriana 40; T. bakeri 40, **41**; T. batalinii 40, **41**; T. flora 39, **41**; T. 'Bronze Charm' 42; T. clusiana & var. chrysantha (T. chrysantha) 39; T. cretica 40; T. eichleri 40; T. fosteriana 40; hybrids 42; T. greigii 40, hybrids **42**; T. hageri 40; T. humilis 40; T. kaufmanniana & hybrids 42, **42**; T. linifolia 42; T. maximowiczii **42**; T. orphanidea 40; T. polychroma 39; T. praestans 40; T. pulchella 40; T. saxatilis 40; T. sprengeri 40, **41**; T. sylvestris 39–40; T. tarda 40; T. dasysteman) 39; T. turkestanica 39, **41**; T. urumiensis 40, **41**; T. violacea & var. pallida 40; T. whittallii 40

Zephyanthes candida 45, **63**
Zigadenus fremontii 61; Z. micranthus 61